D1258942

Emma Stone

By Kelly Spence

Crabtree Publishing Company

Crabtree Publishing Company

www.crabtreebooks.com

Author: Kelly Spence
Publishing plan research and development: Reagan Miller
Photo research: Tammy McGarr
Editor: Kathy Middleton
Proofreader and Indexer: Wendy Scavuzzo
Designer: Ken Wright
Production coordinator and prepress technician: Ken Wright
Print coordinator: Margaret Amy Salter

Photographs:
Alamy: © AF archive: p. 20
Corbis: © infuspa-10/INFphoto.com: p. 26
Everett Collection: © Columbia Pictures: p. 15
Getty Images: Dana Edelson/© NBC/NBCU Photo Bank via Getty Images: p. 18; Stephen Lovekin: p. 24; Kevin Winter: p. 25;
Keystone: ©ZUMAPRESS.com: p. 13 (bottom); © CARV/AKM-GSI: p. 22; © BEImages: pp. 27, 28;
Photofest: Universal Pictures: p. 7 (top); Fox Broadcasting: p. 14; 20th Century Fox: p. 16; Screen Gems: p. 17; © Fox Searchlight Pictures: p. 23
Shutterstock: © carrie-nelson: front cover; © Featureflash: title page, p. 12; © magicinfoto: p. 4; © Everett Collection: p. 5; © Helga Esteb: p. 6; © Neftali: p. 7 (bottom); © s_bukley: p. 13 (top); © Joe Seer: p. 21
Superstock: DREAMWORKS PICTURES, p. 19
Seth Poppel/Yearbook Library: pp. 8, 9, 11
Wikimedia Commons: Public domain: p. 10 (right)

Every effort has been made to trace copyright holders and to obtain their permission for use of copyright material. The authors and publishers would be pleased to rectify any error or omission in future editions. All the Internet addresses given in this book were correct at the time of going to press. The author and publishers regret any inconvenience caused if addresses have changed or sites have ceased to exist, but can accept no responsibility for any such changes.

Library and Archives Canada Cataloguing in Publication

Spence, Kelly, author
    Emma Stone / Kelly Spence.

(Superstars!)
Includes index.
Issued in print and electronic formats.
ISBN 978-0-7787-8078-6 (bound).--ISBN 978-0-7787-8082-3 (pbk.).--
ISBN 978-1-4271-9984-3 (pdf).--ISBN 978-1-4271-9980-5 (html)

    1. Stone, Emma, 1988- --Juvenile literature. 2. Motion picture actors and actresses--United States--Biography--Juvenile literature. I. Title. II. Series: Superstars! (St. Catharines, Ont.)

PN2287.S73S74 2015   j791.4302'8092   C2014-907804-8
                                                    C2014-907805-6

Library of Congress Cataloging-in-Publication Data

Spence, Kelly.
    Emma Stone / Kelly Spence.
        pages cm. -- (Superstars!)
    Includes index.
    ISBN 978-0-7787-8078-6 (reinforced library binding : alk. paper) -- ISBN 978-0-7787-8082-3 (pbk. : alk. paper) -- ISBN 978-1-4271-9984-3 (electronic pdf) -- ISBN 978-1-4271-9980-5 (electronic html)
    1. Stone, Emma, 1988---Juvenile literature. 2. Actors--United States--Biography. 3. Singers--United States--Biography. I. Title.

PN2287.S73S74 2015
791.4302'8092--dc23
[B]
                                                    2015001577

Crabtree Publishing Company
www.crabtreebooks.com   1-800-387-7650

Printed in Canada/042015/BF20150203

Published in Canada
Crabtree Publishing
616 Welland Ave.
St. Catharines, ON
L2M 5V6

Published in the United States
Crabtree Publishing
PMB 59051
350 Fifth Avenue, 59th Floor
New York, New York 10118

Published in the United Kingdom
Crabtree Publishing
Maritime House
Basin Road North, Hove
BN41 1WR

Published in Australia
Crabtree Publishing
3 Charles Street
Coburg North
VIC 3058

CONTENTS

Words that are defined in the glossary are in
bold type the first time they appear in the text.

All Eyes on Emma

Often called Hollywood's "It Girl," Emma Stone is an incredibly successful and talented actor. From her early start in teen comedies such as *Superbad* to dramatic roles in *The Help* and *Birdman*, Emma's acting ability covers an impressive **range**. In just a few short years, she has captured **blockbuster** roles and worked with such **iconic** directors and producers as Woody Allen and Judd Apatow.

Emma signs autographs for excited fans in Moscow at the Russian premiere for *The Amazing Spider-Man* in June 2012.

Doing It All

While Emma has appeared on TV and performed in live theater, movies continue to be her favorite medium, or form, to work in. At the age of 26, she has been nominated for two Golden Globes and an Academy Award (Oscar), recognizing her natural comedic talent and acting skill. She is recognized as someone who takes charge of her career and follows her own path to stardom. Throughout her rise in Hollywood, Emma has stayed true to her values in the roles she takes. She does not bow to the pressures of a movie industry that likes to **typecast** actors in the same role over and over again. Her hard work, down-to-earth attitude, and trademark sense of humor have made Emma one of Hollywood's favorite leading ladies—both on and off the big screen.

Emma is all smiles at the premiere for *Superbad* in July 2008.

She Said It

"I just always thought I'd be a comedian. It was way more important to be funny or honest than to look a certain way."
—Interview on Lynn Hirschberg's Screen Test on *W* magazine online, January 2011

5

Natural-born Talent

Emily Jean Stone was born on November 6, 1988, in Scottsdale, Arizona. Her father Jeff works as a **contractor** and her mother Krista stayed home to raise the children. When Emma was two, her younger brother Spencer was born. She describes herself as a "loud and bossy" child. Her parents were part owners of the Camelback Golf Club, and when Emma was 12, the family actually lived at the club. The family's heritage is Swedish, English, Irish, and Scottish. Emma's grandfather immigrated to the United States through Ellis Island and the family's Swedish last name, Sten, was **anglicized** to Stone. Emma has always been very close to her family, who have supported her throughout her career.

Emma went to the 2012 Academy Awards in Los Angeles, California, with her brother Spencer.

At The Top of Her Lungs!

Emma is known for having a deep, **husky** voice. She believes it developed when she suffered from colic as a baby. Her **vocal chords** were damaged from crying and coughing. She still sometimes loses her voice from talking too much.

The Theater Bug

When she was just four years old, Emma knew one day she wanted to be an actor. Her father loved movies, and she grew up watching and admiring comedians such as Steve Martin and John Candy. The first film to really have an impact on Emma's dream of becoming an actor was the Steve Martin movie *The Jerk*. In the first grade, her teacher encouraged her to be in the school's Thanksgiving play, *No Turkey for Perky*. After the performance, Emma was hooked. She had officially been bitten by the acting bug.

She Said It

"My parents always made me feel as though I could do anything—not in a cheerleading, 'You're the greatest!' kind of way; it was more, 'You're going to have to work hard, but we'll support you however we can.'"
—Interview in *The Daily Mail*, October 10, 2011

Overcoming Anxiety

Always an outgoing kid, Emma suddenly began experiencing panic attacks related to **anxiety** when she was eight. She describes feeling "immobilized" and not wanting to spend time with her friends. But her parents were determined that she not let her anxiety stop her. Emma worked with a therapist until the age of ten to overcome her fears and discovered acting was an outlet for her emotions.

Tech Talk

As a kid, Emma loved technology. She taught herself how to build websites and write HTML coding. She also wrote and designed her own e-zine called *Neptune*.

Emma's sixth grade school picture at Cocopah Middle School

A Natural!

Emma joined the Valley Youth Theater in Phoenix when she was 11. It wasn't long before she landed leading roles in the theater's productions. Her first role was as Otter in *The Wind in the Willows*. Emma's acting teacher, Bobb Cooper remembers recognizing talent right away in the blonde-haired, blue-eyed girl. Between the ages of 11 and 15, Emma starred in 16 shows at the theater, including *The Wizard of Oz* and *The Princess and the Pea*. Emma was always up for a new challenge. Bobb described Emma as very capable and a natural comedian. "Pretty much everything I threw at her she was able to take on. She had a great comedic timing and great sense for comedy."

Emma balanced a normal childhood of attending school with professional training at the Valley Youth Theater.

She Said It

"Comedy was my sport. It taught me how to roll with the punches. Failure is the exact same as success when it comes to comedy because it just keeps coming. It never stops."
—Interview in *Vogue* magazine, June 18, 2012

Center Stage

At the theater, Emma joined an improv troupe. Short for "improvisation," improv is a kind of acting where the story and dialogue are made up on the spot by the actors. Emma took to improv right away with her lightning-quick wit and love of a challenge. She also began watching sketch comedy skits by one of her mother's favorite comedians, Gilda Radner. Emma considers watching these skits on *Saturday Night Live* symbolic of where her dream of becoming a comedian started. She dreamed of one day appearing on the popular live TV show.

Great Gilda

Gilda Radner was an original cast member on *Saturday Night Live*. She created such outrageous characters as teenaged nerd Lisa Loopner and the loudmouthed Roseanne Rosannadanna. Gilda, whom Emma describes as her "original hero," died of ovarian cancer in 1989.

California Dreamin'

One day while sitting in class during the ninth grade, Emma had a brainwave. If she wanted to be a professional actor, she needed to go to Hollywood! She hurried home and set to work creating a PowerPoint presentation. She called it "Project Hollywood 2004" and was determined to use it to convince her parents to let her move to Los Angeles, California. The presentation featured the hit song "Hollywood" by Madonna and pictures of famous actors who had started their careers at a young age. Emma handed her parents a big bucket of popcorn and made her case. It worked! Although she was only 15, Emma and her mother moved west from Arizona to star-studded Los Angeles so Emma could pursue her acting dream.

Homeschooled Emma tried attending school again in her freshman year of high school but went back to being homeschooled after her first semester.

She Said It

*"You know how sports teach kids teamwork, and how to be strong and brave and confident? Improv was my sport. I learned how to not **waffle** and how to hold a conversation, how to take risks and actually be excited to fail. It taught me so much, and helped me overcome so much."*
—Interview on nj.com, July 31, 2011

11

Hello, Hollywood!

In January 2004, Emma and her mother landed in Los Angeles for **pilot** season. Emma rolled up her sleeves and began going to five or six auditions a week. In between auditions, she took high school courses online and worked part-time at a bakery for dogs. Emma is good-natured about the fact that customers said their dogs found the treats she baked inedible. Luckily, for her fans (and dogs everywhere!), Emma decided not to pursue a career at the bakery.

Emma and her mother Krista

What's in a Name?

When Emma registered with the Screen Actors Guild (SAG), there was already an actress named Emily Stone. She decided to register as Riley Stone instead, but the name didn't stick. That's when she officially became known as Emma Stone. She is still called Emily by her family and friends.

Retro Rewind

In 2004, her mother Krista saw an ad calling for contestants for a new reality singing show called *In Search of the New Partridge Family*. Participants would be competing to win roles on a **remake** of the popular 1970s TV show, which starred David Cassidy and Susan Dey. Emma was skeptical but attended auditions and won a spot as a contestant. After six episodes singing songs such as Pat Benatar's "We Belong," Emma was excited to finally win the role of Laurie Partridge. Unfortunately, *The New Partridge Family* never made it past the pilot episode.

Emma's mother thought she looked similar to Susan Dey, the actress who played Laurie Partridge in the original series.

Rock Bottom

The next couple of years proved to be a struggle. In 2006, Emma auditioned for a TV show called *Heroes* and made it to the final round. But when she overheard the show's producers give the role to actress Hayden Panettiere, she felt like she had hit rock bottom. Disappointed, Emma tried not to be too discouraged. After all, she figured there was no way for her to go but up.

Toning It Down

Through her first few years in Los Angeles, Emma experienced some growing pains. Coming from an improv and stage acting background, Emma was used to performing with tons of energy and big expressions. She worked hard to tone down her acting to "a teaspoon from a bucket" to better fit the movie roles she was auditioning for. Emma also never wanted to be typecast based on her appearance. Being taken seriously as a comedian has always been a priority for her before she takes on any new projects.

In *Drive*, Emma's character is surprised to learn she is in a cross-country road race with her father, played by actor Dylan Baker.

Picking Up Speed

In 2007, Emma was cast as Violet Trimble in a new TV action series called *Drive* about competitors in a road race. Again, the job was short-lived and the show was canceled after only seven episodes. But Emma's career was about to take off at top speed.

Super Good!

Soon after *Drive* was canceled, a film script for a new teen comedy called *Superbad* landed in Emma's hands. It was love at first sight. The script came from film producer Judd Apatow who was riding a string of highly successful comedies including *The 40-Year-Old Virgin*. Emma auditioned and was cast as Jules in the film. Filming a movie about high school turned out to be a lot of fun for Emma because she had missed out on the high school experience herself. She became fast friends with her costars Jonah Hill and Michael Cera, and the three young comedians improvised many scenes together. *Superbad* was a runaway hit. People were beginning to take notice of the spunky redhead.

Seeing Red

Emma is a natural blonde but was brown-haired before filming *Superbad*. Judd Apatow had Emma dye her hair red for her role in the movie. Red hair has since become part of her **signature** look.

Emma and her costar Jonah Hill whip up some laughs on the set of *Superbad*.

Bigger and Better

Superbad was a launching pad for Emma. She quickly landed supporting film roles in a number of comedies. She played a band member in *The Rocker*, a sorority girl in *The House Bunny*, a scorned girlfriend in *Ghosts of Girlfriends Past*, and a zombie-slayer in *Zombieland*.

For her role in *The Rocker*, Emma learned how to play bass guitar.

Time for a Change

Emma was now well established as an actress and was finding regular work. But in 2009, she decided it was time to shake things up. After five years in Los Angeles, Emma wanted to live somewhere where every conversation she overheard was not about the movie industry. She decided to move east to the artistic neighborhood of Greenwich Village in the heart of New York City.

Making the Grade

In 2010, Emma auditioned for her first lead role. In the movie *Easy A*, high school senior Olive Penderghast uses the rumor mill to become popular. For her audition, Emma had to perform a **monologue** as Olive on webcam. She nailed it. The movie was a huge box office hit, and popular film critic Roger Ebert declared the role would make Emma Stone a star. He was right. Emma says she loved playing a strong comedic female lead, and her performance earned her a Golden Globe nomination and the award for Best Comedic Performance at the 2011 MTV Movie Awards.

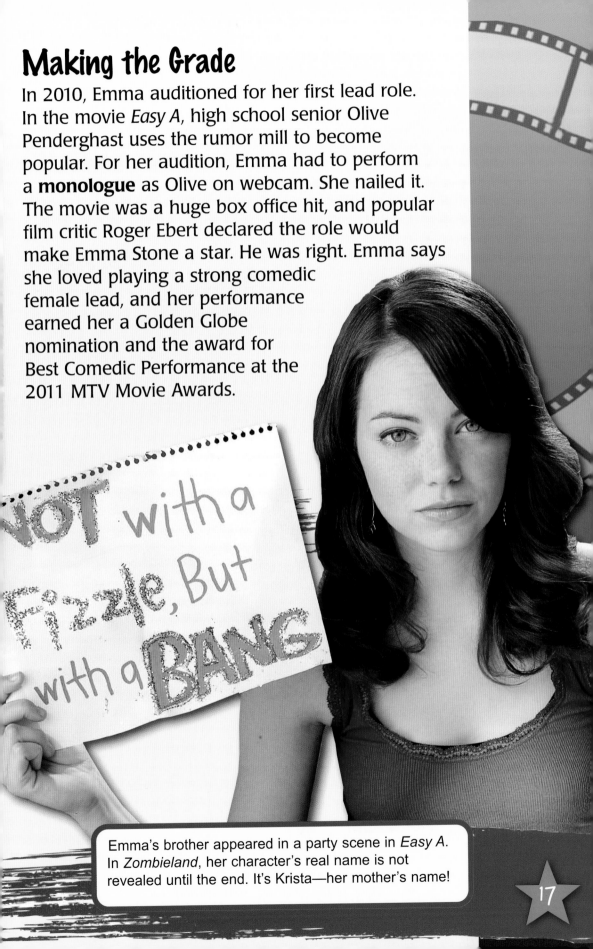

Not with a Fizzle, But with a BANG

Emma's brother appeared in a party scene in *Easy A*. In *Zombieland*, her character's real name is not revealed until the end. It's Krista—her mother's name!

Live From New York!

Riding the wave of her success in *Easy A*, Emma was invited to fulfill a lifelong dream—hosting *Saturday Night Live*. She loved the thrill of performing before a live audience. On the show, she got to do **impressions**, sing, and even dance. She would go on to host the show again the following year, and even make a surprise **cameo** appearance when her boyfriend, actor Andrew Garfield, hosted in 2014.

Emma breaks into a crazy dance in a French teen dance-off on *Saturday Night Live*.

Funny Girl

Cementing her reputation as a superb comedian, Emma starred in 2011 alongside Ryan Gosling and Steve Carell in the romantic comedy *Crazy, Stupid, Love*. In one scene, Emma was supposed to leap up and be lifted over Ryan's head. She tried to perform the jump, but had a panic attack when she flashed back to the time she broke both arms at the age of seven on the parallel bars in gymnastics. In the end, a **stunt double** had to do the scene for her.

The Help

It was her second big movie of 2011 that helped Emma gain attention as a dramatic actress. The much-anticipated movie *The Help* portrayed racial inequality between white families and their maids during the civil rights era. The film is set in Mississippi, so a **dialect** coach helped Emma develop a Southern accent. Emma's mother was raised in Louisiana so she was able to help her practice. After the movie was released, Emma and her costar Octavia Spencer were invited to a private screening of the movie at the White House by First Lady Michelle Obama.

In *The Help*, Emma plays Skeeter, a journalist who secretly writes a book about African American maids in 1960s Jackson, Mississippi.

She Said It

"I hate watching myself on screen, because I only see flaws I wish I could change, but when the First Lady asks you to do something, you've got to make an exception."
—Interview in *Stylist* magazine, 2011

19

Flying High

Emma added a new genre to her skill set in 2012—action! The Spider-Man series was being resurrected and casting was looking for Spidey's new leading lady. Emma won the role of Gwen Stacy, the superhero's first love, in *The Amazing Spider-Man*. During filming, Emma performed some of her own stunts, swinging in a harness 20 feet off the ground. But even as an adult, Emma sometimes still suffers from anxiety. To help herself feel more in control, she baked in her spare time during filming. She also meditates when she starts to feel overwhelmed.

Sign Here!

Emma was so obsessed with the Spice Girls as a child that she even memorized how to do each of the group's autographs!

Spice World

Emma was—and still is—a huge fan of the group the Spice Girls! During a press tour in the United Kingdom for *The Amazing Spider-Man*, she received two special messages—one from Mel B. (Scary Spice) and one from Mel C. (Sporty Spice)!

Web of Love

During filming for *The Amazing Spider-Man*, sparks flew on- and offscreen between Emma and her British-American costar Andrew Garfield. In mid-2011, the two quietly began dating. The couple is notoriously private about their relationship. They live together in New York City with their golden retriever, Ren.

Director Mark Webb noticed "fireworks" between Emma and Andrew during their first audition together.

He Said It

"Working with Emma was like diving into a thrilling, twisting river and never holding on to the sides [...] The only way acting with someone should be."
—Andrew Garfield interview in *Vogue*, June 18, 2012

Gangster Squad

In 2013, Emma paired up again with Ryan Gosling in the crime film *Gangster Squad*. The two costars were excited to work together again, and Ryan admits it was sometimes difficult for the two to focus on serious acting without goofing around. Emma prepared for the film by watching movies from the 1940s, the era in which the story takes place.

Emma strikes a pose alongside one of her costars, Belt the three-toed sloth, at the New York City premiere of *The Croods*.

Dog Days

In 2006, Emma gave voice to a Pomeranian named Ivana on the TV show *The Suite Life of Zack & Cody*. In 2010, she lent her voice again to Mazie, an Australian Shepherd, in the live action film *Marmaduke*.

Emma Stone-Age

Emma returned to cartoon work, providing the voice for a teenaged cavegirl named Eep in the computer-animated movie *The Croods*. She said she had a lot of fun working alongside Nicolas Cage and Ryan Reynolds, but had to be careful not to overdo it and lose her voice. Emma will **reprise** her role as Eep in *The Croods 2*, set for release in 2017.

Take Two

In 2014, it was back to the web for Emma as Gwen Stacy in the **sequel** *The Amazing Spider-Man 2*. Fans loved watching Emma and Andrew reignite their chemistry on screen.

Michael Keaton and Emma in a scene from *Birdman*.

Oscar Talk

The same year, in the romantic comedy *Magic in the Moonlight*, Emma starred alongside British actor Colin Firth as a psychic who predicts the future. She called it a "dream come true" to work with the movie's famous director Woody Allen. Still later that year, Emma took on a challenging dramatic role. In the movie *Birdman*, she plays a recovering drug addict who is resentful and angry at her father. The demanding role was well worth it. Her performance earned her a Golden Globe Award nomination and her first Oscar nomination for Best Actress in a Supporting Role.

Pay It Forward

Emma became the spokesperson for Revlon cosmetics as well as the company's cancer awareness program Revlon Cares in 2012. Her own mother was diagnosed with a hard-to-treat kind of breast cancer. During her treatment, Emma flew home many times to be with her mother. To celebrate two years of Krista being cancer-free, Emma and her mom got matching tattoos inspired by the Beatles' song "Blackbird." The tattoo of bird footprints was actually designed by former Beatle Paul McCartney after Emma wrote him a letter about her mother.

Emma and her mother laced up for the 2013 Revlon Run/Walk to raise awareness for women's health issues.

Gilda's Club

In 1991, Gilda's Club was founded in honor of Gilda Radner as a support center for people living with cancer, as well as their friends and families. Emma is an ambassador, or representative, for the branch located in New York City. She works closely with programs that reach out to kids and teens.

Blazing a Trail

Emma has always focused on being taken seriously as an actor. In 2012, she was recognized with the very first MTV Trailblazer Award. This award is presented to a young actor who has forged his or her own path to stardom and has worked on a wide range of movies. In her acceptance speech, Emma named some of her role models as Gilda Radner, Charlie Chaplin, writer J.D. Salinger, and director Cameron Crowe. She also encouraged everyone to follow their own paths and to be "originals."

An emotional Emma accepts the 2012 MTV Trailblazer Award.

She Said It

"*What sets you apart can feel like a burden. And it's not. A lot of the time it's what makes you great.*"
—Acceptance speech for the Trailblazer Award at the MTV Movie Awards, June 2012

Privacy, Please!

It has always been important to Emma that her personal life remains private, especially her relationships. In September 2012, Emma and Andrew Garfield decided to put their fame to good use. After having lunch in a New York City restaurant, the pair were tipped off that **paparazzi** were waiting outside to take their picture. The photographers were surprised when the couple emerged holding cardboard signs over their faces promoting two charities. The photos went **viral** and other celebrities began to copy their idea.

Emma supports Gilda's Club and Andrew has done public service announcements for the Worldwide Orphans Foundation.

They Said It

"We just found out that there are paparazzi outside the restaurant we were eating in. So, why not take this opportunity to bring attention to organizations that need and deserve it? www.wwo.org and www.gildasclubnyc.org, Have a great day!"—Signs held by Emma and Andrew to promote charities

Emma takes a bow with costar Alan Cumming on her opening night in *Cabaret* in New York City in November 2014.

Treading the Boards

Emma has always loved musical theater. During a trip to New York City when she was nine, Emma saw *Cabaret* on Broadway starring Natasha Richardson. She was mesmerized by the main character Sally Bowles, a nightclub singer in 1930s Germany. Little did she realize that, in 2014, her Broadway dream would become a reality. Emma landed the lead role of Sally Bowles in the **revival** of *Cabaret*. The opportunity brought new challenges for Emma—it was the first time she had done live theater since high school, and it came with a grueling schedule. But with lots of rehearsal and support from the cast, Emma's hard work paid off. Critics heaped praise on her performance.

What's Next?

Next on Emma's agenda is the romantic comedy *Aloha* directed by Cameron Crowe. She plays an air force pilot on a mission with a military contractor, played by Bradley Cooper, to stop a top-secret missile launch. Also in 2015, Emma teams up with director Woody Allen again, starring in the drama-comedy *Irrational Man* with Joaquin Phoenix. As for the future, Emma has said she would love to one day step behind the camera and work as a producer. In the meantime, this superstar actress is soaking up every moment of living out her lifelong dream-come-true, and is following the advice she gave in *Glamour* magazine in 2011: *"You're a human being, you live once and life is wonderful, so eat the...red velvet cupcake."*

She Said It

"I'd like to produce. I'd like to come up with ideas and collaborate with people and directors and writers that I like, be a part of movies that have the same idea that the movies that impacted me have. I'd like to be able to do that for people."
—Interview on cinemablend.com, June 2008

28

Timeline

1988: Emily Jean Stone is born on November 6 in Scottsdale, Arizona

1999: Emma Stone begins acting at the Valley Youth Theater in Phoenix

2003: Emma convinces her parents to let her move to Los Angeles to pursue acting using a PowerPoint presentation

2004: Emma and her mother move to Los Angeles, California

2005-2006: Emma lands small roles on television shows including *In Search of The New Partridge Family*, *Medium*, *The Suite Life of Zack & Cody*, *Malcolm in the Middle*, and *Lucky Louie*

2007: Emma plays Jules in *Superbad*

2008: Emma has supporting roles in *The Rocker* and *The House Bunny*

2009: Emma has supporting roles in *Ghosts of Girlfriends Past*, *Paper Man*, and *Zombieland*, and moves to New York City

2010: Emma lands her first major role in *Easy A*, does voice work in *Marmaduke*, and hosts *Saturday Night Live* for the first time

2011: Emma stars in *Crazy, Stupid, Love*, *The Help*, and *Friends with Benefits*

2012: Emma has leading roles in *The Amazing Spider-Man*, appears on the TV show *iCarly*, and is awarded the MTV Trailblazer Award

2013: Emma voices Eep in *The Croods* and stars in *Gangster Squad*

2014: Emma stars in *The Amazing Spider-Man 2*, *Birdman*, and *Magic in the Moonlight*, and makes her first appearance on Broadway in *Cabaret*

2015: Emma is nominated for a Golden Globe and an Academy Award for Best Supporting Actress for *Birdman;* filming *Irrational Man* directed by Woody Allen and *Aloha* directed by Cameron Crowe

2017: Emma will voice Eep again in *The Croods 2*

Glossary

anglicized To change a foreign word or phrase for use when speaking English

anxiety A feeling of uneasiness caused by fear

blockbuster A motion picture expected to be popular and financially successful

cameo A minor appearance by a well-known actor in a movie or TV show

contractor A person that provides materials or services for a fee

dialect A form of a language that is spoken in a particular area

husky Low and raspy

iconic Important and notable

impressions Impersonations of other people

monologue A long speech given by a character in a story, movie, or play

paparazzi Photographers who take pictures of celebrities

pilot A standalone episode of a show made to sell the show to a TV network

range A wide variety of skill

remake To film again

reprise To repeat

revival A new production of an old play

sequel A movie or book that continues the story of the original

signature A distinguishing style or feature

stunt double A look-alike who performs difficult or dangerous stunts for an actor or actress

typecast To repeatedly assign an actor or actress the same type of role or character

viral Made popular by circulating quickly from person to person, especially through the Internet

vocal chords Two pieces of tissue in the throat that vibrate to make the sound of a voice

waffle To be unable to make up your mind

Find Out More

Books

Rueda, Marty. *Emma Stone*. (Rising Stars). Gareth Stevens Publishing, 2013.

Schwartz, Heather E. *Emma Stone: Star of the Stage, TV, and Film.* (Pop Culture Bios) Lerner Publishing Group, 2014.

Tieck, Sarah. *Emma Stone: Talented Actress.* (Big Buddy Biographies) ABDO Publishing, 2013.

Websites

Emma Stone Biography:
www.biography.com/people/emma-stone-20874773

Emma's biography on People.com
www.people.com/people/emma_stone/biography/

Gilda's Club NYC
http://www.gildasclubnyc.org/Membership/Programs.html

Index

About the Author

Kelly Spence works as an editor and writer in children's publishing. When her nose is not buried in a book, she is either running, trying out a new vegetarian recipe, or spending time with family, friends, and Zoey, her energetic boxer.